STYLE
on a shoestring

ANNE McKEVITT & SHELLEY WARRINGTON

special photography by **COLIN POOLE**

STYLE
on a shoestring

Simple Ideas For Fantastic Rooms

BAY
BOOKS
San Francisco

First published 1997 by Quadrille Publishing Limited, London. North American
edition published 1998 by SOMA Books, by arrangement with Quadrille
Publishing Ltd.

Bay Books is an imprint of Bay Books & Tapes, Inc. Bay Books may be
purchased for education, business, or sales/promotional use at attractive
quantity discounts. For information, address: Bay Books & Tapes, 555
De Haro St., No. 220, San Francisco, CA 94107

For the Quadrille edition:

Publishing Director: **ANNE FURNISS**

Art Director: **MARY EVANS**

Design: **BALLEY DESIGN ASSOCIATES**

SIMON BALLEY & JOANNA HILL

Picture Research: **NADINE BAZAR**

Production Director: **VINCENT SMITH**

For the Bay Books edition:

Publisher: **JAMES CONNOLLY**

Art Director: **JEFFREY O'ROURKE**

Editorial Director: **CLANCY DRAKE**

Cover Design: **CABRA DISEÑO**

Proofreader: **MARIANNA CHERRY**

Library of Congress Cataloguing-in-Publication Data on file with the Publisher

ISBN 0-912333-66-9

Printed in Hong Kong

10 9 8 7 6 5 4 3 2 1

Distributed to the trade by Publishers Group West

contents

 **WELCOME** TO *STYLE ON A SHOESTRING*. COME IN, MAKE YOURSELF AT HOME, AND LEAVE ALL YOUR PREVIOUS

THOUGHTS ABOUT DECORATING OUTSIDE IN THE COLD.  WE WANT TO DISPEL THE

MYTH THAT TO HAVE A STYLISH HOME YOU NEED TO BE RICH. WE HAVE ALL BEEN LED TO BELIEVE THAT THE

MORE YOU SPEND ON A PRODUCT THE BETTER IT IS, BUT THIS IS NOT NECESSARILY THE CASE. DON'T BE CONNED INTO

THINKING THAT EXPENSIVE IS BEST. SOMETIMES, THE DIFFERENCE BETWEEN BASIC PAINT AND EXPENSIVE SPECIAL-EFFECTS PAINT

IS ONLY ONE MAGIC INGREDIENT—WATER! THE SAME GOES FOR A COSTLY KITCHEN VERSUS A LESS EXPENSIVE ONE. THE

# NTROD

DIFFERENCE IS OFTEN NOTHING MORE THAN FANCY HANDLES OR AN EXTRA-SPECIAL COUNTERTOP. WE WILL SHOW YOU IN

THIS BOOK HOW TO ACHIEVE STYLE ON A SHOESTRING.

THE BOOK TACKLES ALL ASPECTS OF HOME DECORATING, AND WE WANT YOU TO FEEL FREE TO EXPERIMENT AND HAVE

FUN. START WITH SOMETHING AS SIMPLE AS A LAMPSHADE, OR TURN AN OLD DOOR INTO A STYLISH

DINING TABLE, CREATE AN INSTANT FOUR-POSTER BED, TRANSFORM A STAIRCASE, OR TURN YOUR BATHROOM

INTO A FANTASY DREAM WORLD. IF YOU'VE NEVER DECORATED BEFORE, DON'T WORRY. WE'LL GIVE YOU THE

CONFIDENCE, WITH EASY-TO-FOLLOW PHOTOGRAPHS, STEP-BY-STEP INSTRUCTIONS, SIMPLE TEXT, AND

READILY AVAILABLE MATERIALS. WE'VE MADE LOTS OF MISTAKES IN THE PAST, BUT YOU DON'T NEED TO: THIS

BOOK IS PACKED FULL OF THE LESSONS WE HAVE LEARNED.

I HAVE A PASSION FOR COLOR. I LIVE AND WORK WITH COLORS INSPIRED BY NATURE: SKY BLUE, SUNNY YELLOW,

FOREST GREEN. THESE ARE THE OPPOSITE OF THE GRAY SKIES, GRAY SEAS AND LONG DARK NIGHTS THAT  I GREW UP

WITH IN THURSO, ON THE NORTHERNMOST TIP OF SCOTLAND.

I HAD ONLY A LITTLE OVER $200 AND LOADS OF VERY INEXPENSIVE IDEAS WITH WHICH TO

DECORATE MY FIRST APARTMENT. FRIENDS STARTED ASKING ME FOR TIPS ON DECORATING, AND, THOUGH SELF-TAUGHT, I

SOON HAD A LARGE NUMBER OF CLIENTS. I BELIEVE THAT IT'S IMAGINATION AND DARING THAT MAKE WONDERFUL INTERIORS,

AND I'M ON A CRUSADE TO RID THE WORLD OF FRILLS, FLOUNCES, AND, CREAM-COLORED WALLS.

UCTION

I HAVE PUT THIS BOOK TOGETHER WITH AN AUSTRALIAN FRIEND SHELLEY WARRINGTON. WE MET WHEN WE WERE

BOTH WORKING IN THE FASHION AND BEAUTY INDUSTRY. OVER DINNER ONE NIGHT, WE BEGAN DISCUSSING THE IMPACT

MY DESIGNS HAD ON FRIENDS AND CLIENTS AND HOW WONDERFUL IT WOULD BE TO SHARE ALL OF THESE IDEAS WITH A

WIDER AUDIENCE. THE IDEA FOR *STYLE ON A SHOESTRING* EVOLVED THAT EVENING AND QUICKLY BECAME THE BOOK

THAT IS IN YOUR HANDS TODAY.

IT'S ALL UP TO YOU NOW. YOU DON'T NEED TRIAL AND ERROR, YOU JUST NEED TO TRY. MAKE COLOR IMPORTANT,

AND REMEMBER THAT MONEY IS NOT. ROLL UP YOUR SLEEVES, PICK UP A PAINTBRUSH, DYE A PILLOW

COVER, WAKE UP YOUR HOME AND MAKE IT FANTASTIC. IT'S AS SIMPLE AS THAT.

inspiration

Take a fresh look at your living room, imagine you've never seen it before, and look closely at all the furniture, knick-knacks, and clutter. What really belongs here? You don't need to buy anything new, just throw out what you no longer like, and customize what you can't do without.

living areas

living
with color

Think of colors that make you happy: blue skies, yellow sunshine, orange sunsets, green forests. Now think of a scheme for your living room. You can use color to change the atmosphere of your room. The enormous range of paints can be intimidating, but don't let choice scare you into choosing cream or off-white. Drab colors are no cheaper than bold ones.

A bold color scheme doesn't always mean color everywhere. Even small amounts of lime and purple make this room bright and colorful.

You can transform an old or second-hand armchair with felt and a length of rope.

Don't throw out small amounts of paint; they may come in handy later. You can often combine different shades in a single project, like this striking multicolored alcove.

These glass doors were livened up using inexpensive sheets of colored tissue paper stuck to clear glass with white glue. The bold effect makes even the hot pink walls and yellow floor look pale.

Mark off a square on your coffee table with masking tape and paint it. Remove the tape and add freehand brushstrokes to the outer edges.

Your choice of colors doesn't need to force you to create a certain style. The same color and similar tones can be used for both a modern and a more classic design.

If you want to rejuvenate a sofa but can't afford upholstery, use a drop cloth. Hardware stores sell 100% cotton drop cloths in cream or beige, but with one pack of fabric dye you can dye them in the washing machine. The fringe can be sewn on later.

In this room, the door and staircase take center stage. If you let one or two big ideas lead a design, the rest of the room should follow.

Use bold furniture and brightly colored tissue paper, stuck to the wall with water-based white glue, to contrast with cream walls and stripped pine floors.

coming up
daisies

Changing the color of your sofa is really no more difficult than changing the color of your walls. This cheap, fun idea began with a drop cloth, a pack of fabric dye, two pounds of salt, and felt for making daisies. Once you get used to the idea that you can't crush the flowers by sitting on them, you won't want to sit anywhere else.

② Cut the templates from the photocopy.

③ Use a pencil to draw around the templates on felt, then cut out the shapes. You need one full daisy for every pillow, plus a pile of leaves.

④ Use bold-colored yarn to sew the felt daisies to the pillows. Huge blanket stitches are easy to sew, and the stitches don't need to be perfect or even.

A sofa can become a sofabed, and sleeping bags can be used as throws.

Glue artificial flowers onto a plain window shade for a different outlook.

stripped
and stunning

Dual-purpose living rooms can be given more than one design. Make your dining space feel different from your sitting space with paint and imagination. The more space you have, the more opportunity there is for creating fun effects.

You can create your own wavy wall from strips of lumber cut to size at the lumberyard. You don't need to call a contractor; just draw a curve along the ceiling and hang the wood from the ceiling with cup hooks.

BEFORE

This Jackson Pollock–style "splattered paint"

rug is fun and easy.

Recycled bottles and a bike wheel make an excellent, cheap light fixture.

Why should chairs always be floor-bound?

This ceiling rosette is painted on freehand, but you could use a pattern or even a stencil.

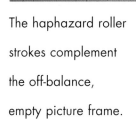

Try this striking animal print stencil (see pages 124–125 for suppliers).

The haphazard roller strokes complement the off-balance, empty picture frame.

Muslin draped over tall chairs instantly creates a theatrical dining room.

new for old

Before you run out and spend money you don't have on furniture you don't need, think about how you can transform the possessions you already own, and make the old look new.

get rid of bookcase

In this room the collections of art were brought together so they stood out, tongue-and-groove flooring was refinished to show off the rug, and the sofa was brought up to date simply by fitting it with feet.

Change to Wooden Venetian blinds

Finish with bold rug

Wall lights instead of ceiling light

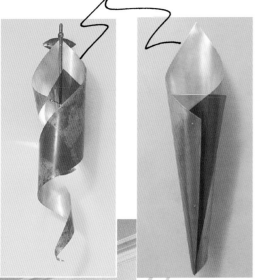

The fireplace was stripped, raised 16 inches, and surrounded with a concrete frame. This is a job for a contractor, but you've saved money by not having to decorate a mantelpiece.

Warm up Wall Color

Raise fire + put in gas log fire

Put down beech floor instead of carpet

Put legs on sofa to update

painted
masterpiece

This room shows what can be achieved on a shoestring budget. Paint was
the only new purchase in the whole transformation.

BEFORE

Mark off squares with masking tape, and paint with a colorwash. The leaf patterns are all stenciled (see pages 124–125 for suppliers). The effect looks terrific, costs almost nothing, and, once you have gathered the full range of colors needed, takes only a few hours.

BEFORE

Removing a door from a cabinet will force you to sort out the hidden clutter.

Throw out the flounce and breathe new life into old curtains or draperies, simply by hanging them properly.

A large floor needs a centerpiece, so if you can't afford a rug, paint your own.

The wood stain on this fireplace looked terrible, and a coat of paint was the only solution. Use black paint on the tiles inside the fireplace to create an illusion of depth, and clear the clutter from the mantelpiece.

BEFORE

roll out the carpet

If you are fed up with rugs buckling underfoot, why not paint your own? First, sand your floorboards, taking special care to vacuum the sawdust; otherwise it will settle on the paint. Then slap on a coat of primer and, once that dries, a base color of your choice.

① Draw your design in pencil.

② You can get perfect straight lines with masking tape.

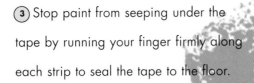

3 Stop paint from seeping under the tape by running your finger firmly along each strip to seal the tape to the floor.

4 Paint in the outer sections of the rug.

5 Let dry, then remove and replace the masking tape so you don't ruin the painting you have already completed; now paint in the central section.

6 Freehand designs and sponge print patterns will bring your rug to life. Finally, varnish with eight coats of acrylic matte varnish.

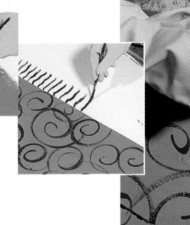

living areas

fantasy
floors

Lurking under the carpet are probably floorboards. They might look dreary when first uncovered, but a coat of paint and a bit of imagination can turn even the grimiest floor into a personal work of art.

THAT WAS THEN

THIS IS NOW

This elegant parquet floor looks stunning with the blue colorwash over it.

TIP

● Always start painting at the wall farthest from the door, and paint your way out of a room. Waiting for paint to dry from an island in the middle of your living room will take all the pride out of your achievement.

Stenciled patterns make excellent floor designs.

This floor has been made out of painted particle board cut into triangles and fitted. It's an inexpensive idea that works especially well in basements, where wood floors are rare, carpet an expensive option, and tiles too cold.

A bold choice of color sets the tone for this room.

door dining

Dining room tables can be expensive, and even the simplest and least attractive tabletop can set you back several hundred dollars. Doors, however, can be turned into unique designer tables for less than the cost of the dinner served on them.

Paneled doors are excellent for displaying small objects, like these keys. You can also stencil keyholes on your walls and glue photocopies of antique keys to the wall above the wainscoting.

If you can draw, turn your table into a canvas. If not, cut pictures out of books or magazines and stick them on with white glue. Just remember, the more coats of varnish you apply, the longer your artwork will last.

a cut above
the rest

This design uses nothing more expensive than paint and colored paper. The table legs are made from inexpensive wood doweling cut to size at a lumberyard.

① Give the door a coat of acrylic primer, then apply two coats of latex flat paint in a bold color.

TIPS

● Instead of colored paper, use photographs, foreign money, magazine covers, playing cards, color photocopies, prints, maps, comics, postcards, old birthday cards, or tissue paper.

● If you're not sure you want a whole table in this design, try it out with a placemat or tray.

② Mark a 4-inch border around the edge of the table.

③ Cut up as many triangles of colored paper as you need to cover the tabletop. This design uses six colors, but the table still gives an impression of being mainly purple with a bright pattern.

④ Stick the triangles to the table with water-based white glue. Use straight edges along the border, then fill in the center.

⑤ Once the glue has dried, apply two coats of acrylic satin varnish to protect your design.

piano piece

This solid-looking table is made from a thin sheet of plywood cut to the shape of a piano and painted black. Bending a second sheet of wood around the thin top created an impression of depth.

The keyboard design can be used to enhance an ordinary rectangular table. Photocopy and use along one side of the table.

Use a candle to singe the edges of sheets of music for your placemats. Take the sheets to a printer or copy center, laminate them, and they will last forever.

You can use this keyboard template for your own tabletop. You will probably need to enlarge this design to the right size as you photocopy it. Once you have enough sheets to cover one side of your table, use white glue to stick the paper to the table, let dry, and finish with four coats of gloss acrylic varnish.

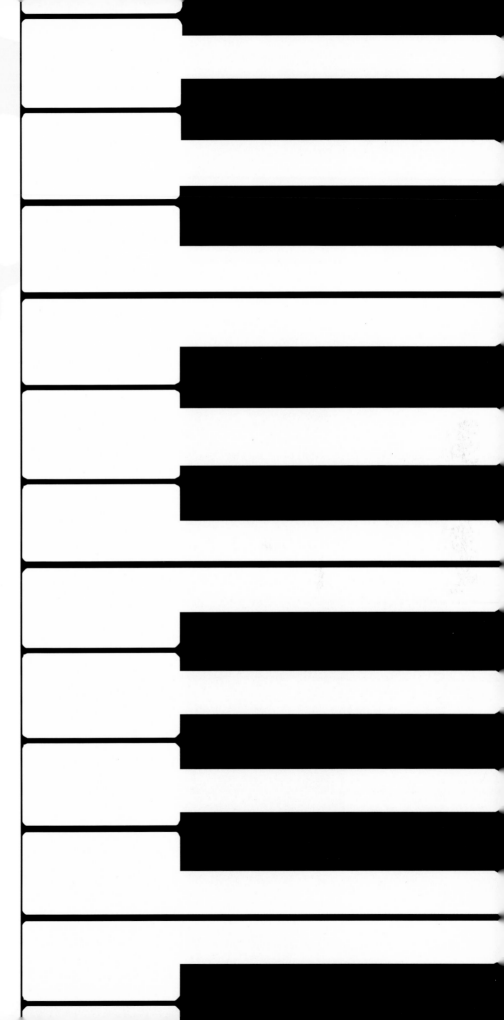

inspiration

K

ITCHENS MUST BE

FUNCTIONAL, BUT YOU MAY ALSO WANT

TO EAT AND RELAX THERE. THINK FIRST

ABOUT HOW YOU COOK AND WHERE

YOU WILL EAT, AS WELL AS WHO HELPS

COOK AND WHO DINES WITH YOU AND

THEN DESIGN YOUR KITCHEN.

kitchens

clever curves

This was once a narrow, dead-end kitchen with no window. Install daylight bulbs on a time switch behind a wall of glass blocks to flood your kitchen with daylight, just during daylight hours. You can also cut diamond-shaped holes in your kitchen wall to let in extra light. Install a curved countertop to transform a once useless corner into valuable cooking space.

kitchens

This floor mosaic made from broken tiles adds texture to the flat clean surfaces elsewhere in the room.

If you have always dreamed of a space-age kitchen, then think metallic. This kitchen looks modern and stylish, without feeling clinical, through the clever use of curved lines. Mixing straight and curved lines adds interest to a room.

TIPS

● A breakfast bar is a wonderful way of adding to your cooking space.

● You could create the metallic look of this kitchen with silver spray paint.

A section of curved countertop can make your kitchen more interesting as well as give you extra storage space.

kitchen
creation

This entire kitchen has been created for $1,200. The secret is to buy the most inexpensive do-it-yourself kitchen set and customize. The only other necessities are paint and lots of imagination.

A stencil has been used to create the effect of a mosaic backsplash. However, it is the final coat of varnish that really deceives the eye. Capture the glossy finish of a real mosaic with satin-finish acrylic varnish; cover the rest of the wall with matte varnish.

kitchens

Sand the cabinets to give the paint a "tooth" to stick to. The heat and steam in a kitchen make it necessary to use oil-based paint on the cabinet doors. Use a small roller for a smooth, professional finish.

TIPS

● If the do-it-yourself kitchen cabinets come with ordinary handles, change them to make your kitchen look elegant.

● There's no need to redo a kitchen completely if it is just the existing doors you're unhappy with; paint them or get a carpenter to make new doors.

BEFORE

Dish towels make ideal covers for small pillows.

Use old utensils to create your own art. Glue-gun whisks, wooden spoons, and a frame to the wall, then paint.

Use paint to bring an old fireplace up to date.

optional
extras

Most kitchen cabinets are plain, but they can be made personalized with
a bit of daring. Don't go for run-of-the-mill backsplashes to protect your
walls; be adventurous and use unusual
materials.

Don't be afraid to use oversized handles on

kitchen cabinets. Textures and colors will

add interest to tiles.

Paint the doors and backsplashes in a light color, then use masking tape to make two different widths and paint with a darker color.

These cabinets were sprayed with metallic blue spray paint, then sheets of stainless steel were stuck to the insides of the panels with special glue. A spray-painted metallic silver backsplash and large chrome handles all help to create a modern look.

kitchens

Stretch loosely woven sacking across kitchen cabinets and apply spray paint from a distance. When the paint is dry, remove the sacking, and you will be left with patterned cabinet doors. Wooden spoons can be screwed to the unit for handles. The backsplash is painted corrugated plastic.

The white tile backsplash has been sponged in rainbow colors using oil-based paint. Do a freehand design on the doors for an individual touch.

Fit corrugated cardboard or plastic into the panels of ordinary cabinets and paint with metallic copper paint. Spigots make unusual handles.

About $225 was all it cost to transform this kitchen into a sunny room. Bold yellows and bright oranges are especially good choices for painting kitchens with no natural light. Paint will brighten up cabinets, walls, floors, and even the refrigerator.

You can laminate sheets of wrapping paper at a printer or copy center and fix them to cabinet doors with wooden beading.

TIP

● Use a metal primer on the refridgerator before applying the top color.

Corner tables take up virtually no space, yet they can transform the way you use a kitchen, or at least the way you eat breakfast.

Inexpensive shelves can be made from plywood and painted in a color that contrasts with the walls.

behind
closed doors

Storage rules this kitchen, with units stretching from floor to ceiling. Think of storage as being either open—that is, with contents displayed on shelves—or closed, with goods tucked away in cabinets and closets. Plates and glasses often look great on open shelves, but old pans are best kept out of sight.

BEFORE

A strip of marble set into the floor at an angle not only adds color to the room but, more important, deceives the eye into believing that the room is wider than it actually is.

This kitchen is clean and uncluttered because all the storage features are hidden behind closed doors. Even the island work station houses a recycling center for glass, paper, plastic, and cans.

The stereo, the wine, and the telephone all help to make the kitchen one of the friendliest rooms in the house.

Here, the shape of the island has provided inspiration for the pattern on the linoleum floor.

Get a carpenter to build an island work station in the middle of a large kitchen to provide work space and a focus for the design.

no space
no waste

Many homes and apartments these days have open-plan living areas, with kitchen and family room—or even living room—combined. If space is limited, the kitchen can seem obtrusive. Fortunately, there are ways to give it a lower profile.

In a small kitchen, you will need to be organized and keep clutter to a minimum. Think carefully about the available space, and take time to plan your layout.

Here, the use of a banister, a raised floor, and different flooring have created a cozy corner kitchen.

TIPS

● Kitchens in open-plan areas need strong extractor fans.

● Separate lighting for this kind of kitchen will allow you to make the kitchen disappear at night when you are in your living space.

● The stove should be fitted into the countertop, allowing space on each side for a preparation area.

● If you find you are walking around your refrigerator to open it, then your door opens the wrong way. Most models are adaptable, so you can rehang the door by moving the hinges to the opposite side.

Don't think your kitchen will disappear if you choose cabinets the same color as the walls. It won't—you will just have a dull kitchen.

A solid storage unit with a front 12 inches higher than the work surface has been built to keep prying eyes out of the kitchen. Because of this, messes can be left in and around the sink until you are ready to deal with it.

kitchens

TIP

● Just because some items are fixed to a wall doesn't mean they can't be removed. Be prepared to move or remove a radiator or air-conditioning unit to free wall space in a small kitchen.

spring cleaning

When your kitchen looks as bad as this one did and you've decided to get a new set of cabinets, make the most of the opportunity and transform the room. It's not every year you install a new kitchen.

BEFORE

While factory-made storage units make the kitchen a pleasure to work in, fun details make it a pleasure to look at. Zinc backsplashes are inexpensive, and a plywood design glued to the wall adds interest.

TIPS

● Distinguish between the eating and cooking areas in a combination kitchen and dining room by painting the floor in each space a different color.

● Why hot water heaters were ever left uncovered is a mystery. Of course you do need access and good ventilation, but inexpensive cabinet doors and a coat of paint will remove the eyesore from sight.

A garden trellis makes an excellent gallery space for kids' paintings, which can be held in place with clothespins.

BEFORE

Screw on fallen branches to make handles.

This tired kitchen table has been revamped with a coat of paint, a leaf print stencil, and plenty of acrylic varnish.

inspiration

Y

OU CAN'T HELP FEELING SORRY

FOR THE ENTRYWAY; FOR TOO LONG IT

HAS SIMPLY BEEN THE PLACE PEOPLE

PASSED THROUGH ON THEIR WAY TO

SOMEWHERE MORE INTERESTING. BUT

THE ENTRYWAY IS THE LAST PLACE YOU

SEE AS YOU LEAVE HOME IN THE MORN-

ING AND THE FIRST SPACE TO WELCOME

YOU BACK AT THE END OF THE DAY, SO

IT DESERVES SPECIAL TREATMENT.

entryways

spare change

We had only $60 to remodel this hallway. The hall had no fewer than nine doors leading from it, and many doors painted one color and the walls another created an eyesore. Painting from floor to ceiling with one color camouflaged the doors and gave it a more uniform look.

BEFORE

Two coats of turquoise latex paint provided a really rich base color. With an ordinary sponge, streaks of violet, mustard, and white paint were smeared over everything. This is fun to do and will change your hallway into a room in its own right.

T I P

● When applying paint streaks, finish all the walls with one color first, then allow this to dry before starting on the next color. This will prevent different colors from running into one another.

The paint came in under budget, by about $3. If you find you have some spare change left over, why not varnish it to the floor for a joke and watch as your friends try to pick it up!

Be extravagant with a big mirror to complete your hallway.

go with
the flow

Don't always think in straight lines. The introduction of curves to the wall, floor, or steps in an entryway or hall will make the space more interesting and disguise what might otherwise be a dull, narrow area.

A curved rug in a hallway will stop you from thinking of the entrance merely as the area at the bottom of the stairs. If you can't find a rug you like, design one yourself and take measurements and sketches to a carpet workroom.

(See pages 124–125.)

Use bent copper piping to create an unusual hall-way light. An electrician will need to wire this for you.

Disguise an ugly radiator with a cover. This one takes its inspiration from the Manhattan skyline. Raid a chemistry set for individual test tube vases to hang above it.

Once this was just an ordinary entryway, but now, with curves, it's a stylish, flowing hall. You lose a corner, but can gain a wonderful alcove for greetings and farewell conversation. Cut floor tiles to emphasize the curved effect.

three-way stairway

A stairway is an opportunity to express your individuality. Think of a theme or design idea and go for it.

The African design was inspired by tribal carvings and uses earthy colors. The Calypso design began with the diamond-shaped border. Don't be afraid to decorate a large space with colors chosen to complement one small detail. The 1950s Hollywood design started with a can of gold spray paint, a great way to glamorize banisters, furniture, or accessories.

CALYPSO

Hang small photographs or prints above a staircase; it is the best way to view them. Paint stairs and the floor with peach, then put on a scarlet colorwash and varnish.

You can find similar African designs in any library. Don't copy any design precisely, as this kind of art shouldn't be too exact.

Finger painting is an easy way to jazz up a stairway. Don't be afraid to add small patches of different colors, like this indigo blue.

AFRICAN

Stick torn strips of tissue paper to any wall with spray glue, then coat with matte varnish. Use a gold marker pen to write on the wall; if your handwriting isn't great, get a friend to help you out. Paint a carpet runner on your stairs, use a stenciled design to cover the "runner," then protect it with acrylic varnish.

HOLLYWOOD

outdoors indoors

Niches exist only for decoration and display. Use a strong color as a backdrop for favorite things, or try a paint effect to echo decorative ideas you are using elsewhere.

You could try floor tiles on your stairs. The cobalt blue looks striking with the contrasting earthy colors of terra-cotta and copper.

TIP

● Slate tiles look and feel great. They bring millions of years of earth history into your home. However, slate is very absorbent and needs to be sealed with wax every six months.

If you long for lush, green pastures, you can buy moss from a florist and stick it to a radiator cover with white glue. Here, the radiator grille is made from an ordinary garden trellis.

Fake ivy hung around the stairwell and decorative branches add to the outside-in effect.

inspiration

Bathrooms are about escape, a chance to pamper yourself and have some peace and quiet. Take a good look at your bathroom, and customize: paint, tile, or change it in any way you can imagine to make it more an expression of your personality.

bathrooms

flying high

Bathrooms can be themed more easily than larger rooms. Take one item you love, such as a print, painting, or photograph, and use these colors and textures throughout the room.

Here, the walls have been colorwashed, and strips of wood were painted to match the towels in the framed print.

SUN & SAND

If you paint radiators the same color as the wall they will be less of an eyesore.

It's often cheaper to re-enamel your bathtub than to replace it.

Use sheets of wood to make a window frame, changing the shape of the window and making it a feature.

NEOCLASSICAL

Real sandstone tiles look great but are expensive. As usual, there is a cheaper way — colorwash. Lay wood tiles and paint on a base coat of cream, then wash on a top coat of sandy-colored latex flat paint, followed by several coats of varnish.

TIPS

● Not only are wood tiles less expensive than stone, but they also feel warmer, especially on bare feet.

● When using paint to imitate sandstone, slate, or marble, colorwash each wood tile as a separate piece of stone. Don't let the paint overlap from one tile to another.

centuries apart

Decorating your bathroom doesn't mean you have to replace the bathroom fixtures. You can achieve a Victorian mood or a modern feel by changing nothing more expensive than paint and wallpaper.

The rich deep colors make this bathroom feel majestic.

If you have a Victorian bathtub, you can make it unique by painting the exterior with oil-based paint.

The stencil pattern on the panels also sets this room firmly in the Victorian era.

Or you can treat the same space and accessories with different paint to make the room feel modern and airy. This color scheme was chosen to complement the wallpaper border.

Stenciled "tiles" cost a fraction of the price of real tiles. Seal with many layers of acrylic varnish.

tile style

This bathroom began life as a closet. If your bathroom is too narrow for a bathtub, yet you long for a soak, try a Japanese tub—ideal if you thought you had space only for a shower.

If you want to tile a curved surface, mosaic tiles are the perfect choice. Fix the mosaic sheets to the plywood with tile adhesive, then grout, just as you would ordinary tiles.

BEFORE

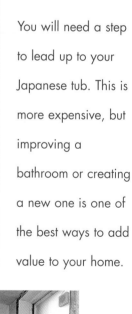

You will need a step to lead up to your Japanese tub. This is more expensive, but improving a bathroom or creating a new one is one of the best ways to add value to your home.

67

(1) Mosaics aren't always tricky. The lazy way to design patterns is to use mosaic tiles, available in 1 foot square and 1 x 2–foot sheets.

(2) If the tiles you are using have a protective paper covering, draw your design on this. Then cut out using scissors.

TIPS

● Sheets of mosaic tiles are also sold with a mesh backing. This is placed directly onto the adhesive-covered surface.

● Use a damp sponge instead of a spatula to apply grout.

● Add a border of mosaic tiles to your existing bathroom tiles.

bathrooms

(3) Check that your design is correct before you fix the tiles to the wall.

(5) Arrange the tiles on the wall and let dry for 24 hours.

(6) Use a wet sponge to dampen the backing sheet, then peel it away from the tiles.

(4) Apply adhesive straight to the tiles to prevent it from getting onto parts of the wall that are not to be covered with mosaic.

(7) Sponge on grout, wiping off any excess with a damp rag.

making waves

Most people have chrome fittings and straight lines, so be different—have your bathroom fittings electroplated, or use curves and wave shapes to make your bathroom special.

An electroplater can plate your existing bathroom faucets in any metal finish, such as copper. Ask for the plating to be sealed so you won't have to worry about tarnish. Pewter, brass, gold, and brushed nickel all make excellent plating finishes.

This chic copper sheet has been curved to screen off the toilet area, making the bathroom more elegant.

Using a jigsaw, cut plywood into waves that can be glued along the front and top of the tub. Create an ocean effect on the floor. Have large sheets of plywood cut into tiles, and paint them with a turquoise and white colorwash, then varnish for protection.

stroke
of genius

It's not essential to use tiles and water-resistant wallpaper in a bathroom. If you really want to give your bathroom a treat, use inventive paint techniques.

① You can use bronze metallic paint as a base for a striking lattice design.

② To get a textured finish, use irregular brushstrokes at first, then finish with strokes in one direction.

TIPS

● If you are using metallic paint, make sure the room is well ventilated; open every window and door you can. You should also wear a mask.

● It is advisable to use extra coats of acrylic varnish around the sink and bathtub.

③ Use latex flat paint to make irregular vertical and horizontal dashes across the wall. Slowly lift the brush from the wall as you reach the end of each stroke for a perfect effect.

④ Allow the first color to dry, then repeat with the second and third colors.

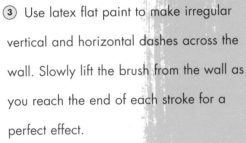

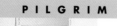

BLOCKED

Let your imagination run wild. A bold color with a block-painted border in contrasting white looks striking.

PILGRIM

CHECKERBOARD

SCRUNCHED

To camouflage uneven wall surfaces, scrunch up a plastic bag, dip it into a darker paint, and press over the lighter-colored base coat.

MIDNIGHT BLUE

When painting a checkerboard design, use masking tape to achieve straight lines. Midnight blue looks best when sealed with a coat or two of gloss acrylic varnish.

TISSUE

COLORWASH

GILT

Unusual colors, shapes, and materials, like torn tissue paper, will liven up any bathroom. Apply extra varnish to areas likely to get wet.

PSYCHEDELIC

MAJESTIC

going
overboard

A small bathroom is the ideal place to develop a theme and let your imagination run wild. Go over the top with accessories like these toy sea creatures; be daring and try colors that you wouldn't normally use; splurge on a great mirror, and paint shapes on the floor.

Drape netting behind the mirror and entangle crabs, lobsters, and fish in it to give the bathroom an undersea feel.

The wave-shaped, cork backsplash was cut with scissors and sealed with acrylic varnish.

If your bathroom looks timid and too small, paint it in bold colors and the room will stand out as if it were twice the size.

BEFORE

Glossy paint gave this bathroom an institutional look; with a change of color and a less shiny finish it has been revitalized.

Hang your odds and ends on a neat row of pegs.

Wrap a length of fake suede around the sink to hide the pedestal and create storage space.

inspiration

B

EDROOMS SHOULD BE

ENTICING, WHETHER YOU WANT

COMFORT, SOLITUDE, OR FUN. WE

SPEND A THIRD OF OUR LIVES IN BED,

SO IT'S WORTH THE TIME AND EFFORT

TO CREATE A ROOM IN WHICH YOU ARE

HAPPY TO RELAX, RESTORE YOUR

ENERGY, AND WAKE UP.

bedrooms

grand
illusions

Too much white can feel clinical and cold, but use this color well and it will look calm, simple, and sophisticated.

BEFORE

The budget for transforming this room allowed only for paint and lining material. Furniture and a headboard painted the same color as the sheets will pull the color scheme together.

Cut ribbon to varying lengths and attach to the top of the curtain for a cascading effect.

Use gold chain hung from cup hooks in the ceiling to suspend a drapery pole in the air.

The secret to a striking black and white room is to use lots of black, but keep each bit small. The harlequin design, stripes, and stencils all provide contrast in a white room without creating pools of darkness.

This hearth has been stenciled, a low-budget alternative to tiles. A touch of greenery will bring a black and white room to life.

bedrooms

the no-poster four-poster

The no-poster four-poster is one of the most elegant ways to turn a nap into true beauty sleep. It's inexpensive, simple, and romantic without being too feminine. Once the rings are in place you can change the fabric as often as you like; try inexpensive muslin or dress lining for the summer, and velvet or brocade for cooler nights.

You need eight lengths of fabric for the draperies. Four lengths will drop from the ceiling to the floor and need to be a yard longer than the height of your room. Two other lengths each need to be one yard longer than the length of your bed, and the final two lengths should be a yard longer than the width of the bed.

A hope chest or blanket box can be painted with crackle glaze and finished with a fleur-de-lis stencil.

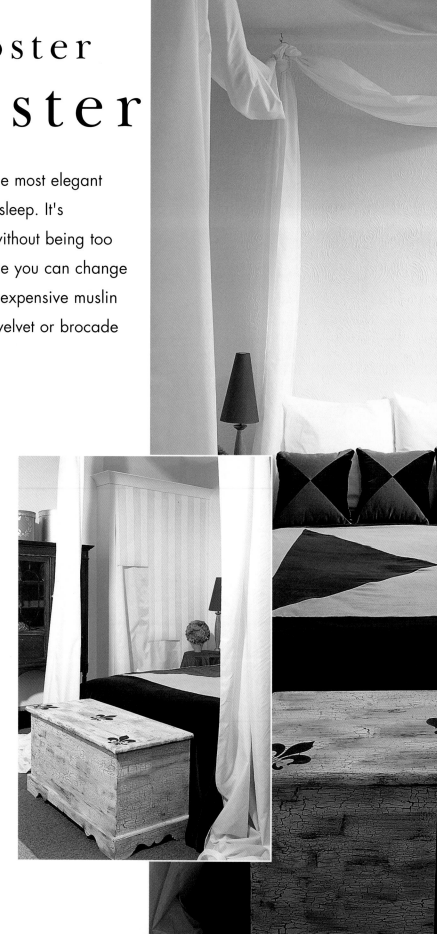

b e d r o o m s

① Bore four holes, one above each corner of the bed. They need to be large enough to accommodate a ¼-inch-wide, 1¼-inch-deep anchor.

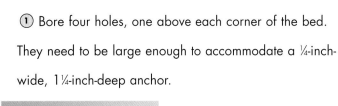

② Use a hammer and screwdriver to tap a plastic anchor into each hole. Anchors are vital, as they provide a strong grip for the hooks and can support the material.

③ Choose the size of the hook to fit the anchor, and twist the hook up into the anchor until it fits snugly and won't go farther without forcing.

④ Fix a ring to each hook. If you want to hang bulky material, use a large ring.

⑤ The excess length gets used up as you knot the fabric to the rings. The fabric hangs from ring to ring, or falls from ceiling to floor with style.

a touch of the
unexpected

The temptation can be to play it safe, but experimentation can really pay off, and the bedroom is a great place to try out ideas that are for your eyes only. These two rooms look sumptuous, yet the budgets from which they were created were modest.

The raspberry stripes and violet bedspread in this room look stunning, and the transparent window curtain hung from the rail adds to the romance. For a bit of old world glamour, get a carpenter to make a canopy support and add draperies of soft muslin.

A piece of sheer voile pierced with imitation flowers makes an unusual headboard centerpiece for this room.

Use the colors of your bedspread to inspire your choice of flower.

out of
the closet

Be creative about your use of space, and if there is a chance of conjuring an extra bedroom out of a closet, then wave that wand.

This was a walk-in closet with no natural light. To let in some light, one door was replaced with translucent glass that has a leaf motif etched into it. A large mirror maximizes the available light and space.

BEFORE

Clever use of hanging storage and a fold-up futon provide extra floor space.

Sloping sides and a curved top make a showpiece of this grape-colored cabinet.

The handles are cut from plywood and fixed to the cabinet doors with carpenter doweling and two screws.

Wardrobes, and especially wardrobe doors, need not be rectangular and dull. It is no more expensive to make a curvy door than a straight one.

baby steps

Please, please, please don't paint your nursery in pastel shades. Babies can see only bold colors; so the niceties of soft pink and "baby" blue are lost on very young eyes. If you want a nursery to stimulate your child, use strong colors and reflective surfaces, preferably lots of them.

Babies spend many of their waking hours gazing at the ceiling. An expanse of white is not going to stimulate their curiosity.

Hang a wood ring from cup hooks screwed to the ceiling, then dangle flowers, bells, and toys from it.

This storage unit was once plain, dull, and doorless. Ask a carpenter to cut and install doors to suit your design ideas. Use several different colors for visual excitement.

T I P

● Varnish the walls even if you have wallpaper — one coat and you'll never worry about grubby little hands.

Spray glue onto a square of aluminum foil and position it on the wall for added sparkle.

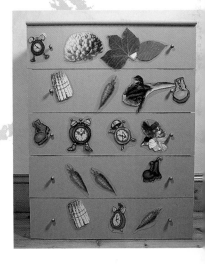

Velcro and laminated giftwrap are used so that children can move the cutouts around.

kids on the go

Don't waste money on expensive children's furniture that your kids will grow out of. Instead, buy standard furniture and adapt it as they get older. The must-have design of one year will be out of date twelve months later.

These shelves are fine for stuffed toys, but one day they will hopefully be used for files and textbooks. The bottom shelf is deep enough to use as a desk.

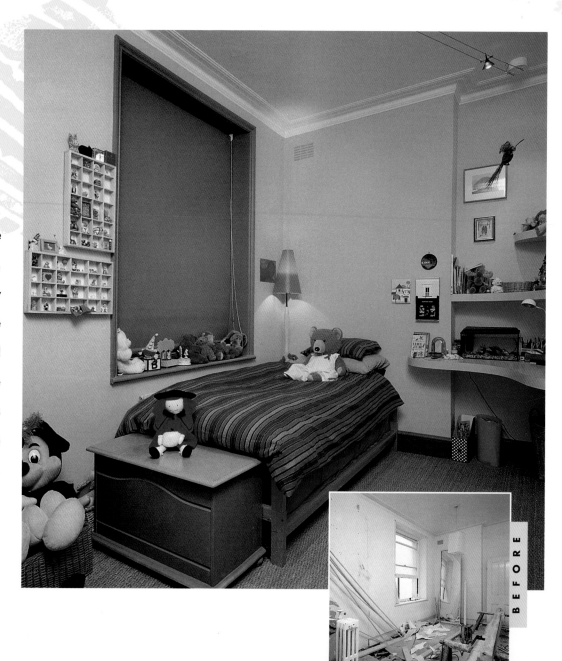

BEFORE

Teenagers' bedrooms are their own private domain, so

let them make their own design choices.

TIP

● Make sure you have ample storage for a T.V., stereo, and computer.

A dress form is a clever way to persuade kids not to throw clothes on the floor. A sari makes an excellent curtain, and painting the inside of the shelving unit a different color from the rest of the walls breaks up the lime color.

jazz up
your bedroom

This transformation cost about $270. Thinking first about space and the use of a room is better than simply going out and spending money.

BEFORE

Make the best of those parts of a room you can't stand, or replace them. The ugly, boxed-in fireplace was painted a different color from the walls and became the headboard.

For extra closet space, make a stylish frame from plywood and hang a cane shade for a door. A colorful rug with a bold pattern will distract the eye from a dull, worn carpet.

If you need a desk but don't have the space, try a fold-down kitchen table.

The window is
dressed with strips of
felt tied with ribbon.

BEFORE

The abstract design on the wall behind the bed was achieved using
paint rollers of varying widths. This design was carried through to
the bedspread using synthetic suede for a fashionable look.

Who needs handles with all these holes to pull? Update plain doors
with holes cut with a jigsaw and backed with dyed muslin.

inspiration

A PIECE OF FURNITURE CAN OFTEN MAKE OR BREAK THE LOOK OF A ROOM. INSTEAD OF SPENDING MONEY ON A PIECE OF PRODUCTION-LINE FURNITURE, BUY CHEAP OR SECONDHAND PIECES AND ADD YOUR OWN TOUCH OF STYLE.

chairs &things

lights, camera, action

Lampshades can be expensive for what is no more than a piece of fabric wrapped around a wire frame. The lamps themselves can also cost more than they should. Buy a basic lampshade and base, then paint and glue on objects to create something special. If you need to, protect your work with a coat of matte acrylic varnish.

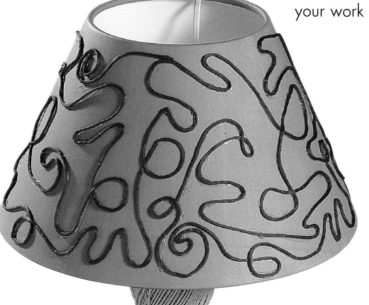

Balls of string have been slipped over the base and a pattern of string glued to the shade.

Once you have finished drawing a design on your shade you can use markers to decorate the base.

Raid the garden for design inspiration and wrap twigs around the lamp stand. The shade here is decorated with fake leaves.

① Use markers to draw even stripes all around the lamp.

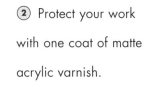

② Protect your work with one coat of matte acrylic varnish.

Stamps can be stuck to a shade with white glue.

Use bangles, necklaces, and fuchsia latex flat paint to enhance a basic lamp.

Use stick-on appliqué motifs, available from the notions section of fabric stores.

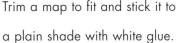

Trim a map to fit and stick it to a plain shade with white glue.

sitting pretty

For some reason the one seat guaranteed to be used every day is rarely decorated. The most popular seat in the house should be made to feel special, so why not draw a design freehand or stencil it with latex flat or spray paint?

You will need to lightly sand a plain wood seat with fine sandpaper to give the paint a surface to bond to. Varnish your design to protect it.

Stores offer a limited selection of towel racks, but it's amazing what you can do with some rope, copper piping, a ladder, and some plastic tubing.

Protect your towels from rust marks by sealing all metals with varnish.

chairs
'n' shelves

Secondhand chairs can be bought for a few dollars. Don't be put off by their color or shabby condition. With a coat of paint and a piece of fabric you can breathe new life into any chair.

First choose a piece of fabric for the seat pad and then decide on a color and design for the frame.

Used chair seat pads tend to be old fashioned, but they are very easy to update. Lift the cushion out of the chair, wrap material around it, tack or staple the fabric in place, and, finally, trim off any excess fabric.

A chair of the past becomes a chair of the future with a coat of paint, 20 yards of ribbon, and a silver seat pad.

TIPS

● When looking at used chairs, keep an eye out for good shapes and solid construction. Avoid anything that creaks, rocks, or has woodworm.

● If the seat pad on the chair you love is beyond repair, cut fireproof foam to shape and cover it.

FRUIT SALAD

AFTERNOON TEA

SOAP OPERA

SCHOOL'S OUT

Ugly mess belongs in closets and cabinets, hidden from sight. Shelving, however, is storage on view. You should use your shelves as much for display as for storage. Make the most of this opportunity to show off your favorite things.

Decorating the front of your shelves with fake flowers, cake pans, nailbrushes, thumbtacks, burlap, and bottle tops gives the dreariest shelf a life of its own.

bookcase
bonanza

A bookcase shouldn't be restricted to housing only books. Versatility is the name of the game. Buy an inexpensive plywood bookcase and then transform it to suit its purpose and surroundings.

A painted cactus design and rope handles give this bookcase-turned-cabinet a Western feel. Terra-cotta pot feet add height and complete the design.

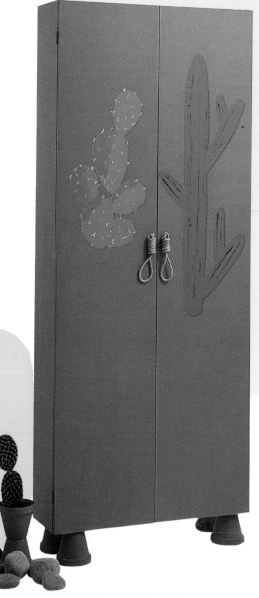

Many home centers sell plaster cornicing, which can be added to the top of your bookcase. Dress fabric—less expensive than upholstery material—is an excellent way to cover kitchen shelves.

Add feet and plaster cornicing to a basic unit, then attach a single door and paint. Rule on fake drawers with a marker, and glue on tassels bought from a notions department.

Fake fur was glued to the bookcase doors and the cow motif reinforced with plywood horns, cloven "feet," and lasso handles.

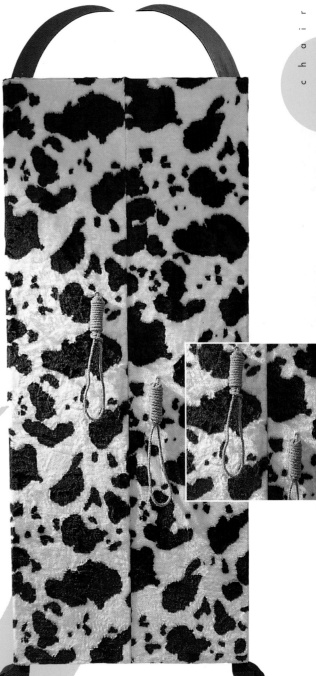

Corrugated cardboard can be painted with several colors, then cut to frame the bookshelves to provide a stylish frame. The cardboard is simply stuck to the edges of the bookcase with double-sided tape.

You don't need to be an artist to transform a bookcase. Copy one of our designs or try one of your own.

Paint and plaster cornicing are an easy way to add unique style to a cheap bookcase.

Get a buzz out of stenciling with this bee design.

Mounting a bookcase on feet can make an enormous difference to a piece of furniture. Plywood doors transform a humble bookcase into a cabinet. Paint and a gold graphic motif complete the transformation.

Cornicing, feet, and doors make the unit look solid. Door handles and gingham fabric give the bookcase a country feel.

Dramatic black and white or tartan ribbons make the original bookcase almost unrecognizable. A length of unbleached muslin can be turned into a makeshift shade.

A length of muslin dress fabric and pompons attached to the shelves turn a bookcase into excellent toy storage.

crackle-glaze cabinet

① Apply a coat of primer, then latex flat paint in the color you wish to show through the cracks.

② Paint on crackle glaze haphazardly.

③ When the glaze has dried, paint a top color of latex flat over it, and watch the cracks appear.

④ Once the paint is completely dry, pick out any extra detail with copper paint. Finish with two coats of acrylic varnish.

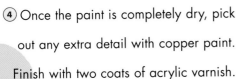

TIP

● Lay the object flat to minimize the chance of the top coat slipping down the unit as it dries.

chairs & things

in the
frame

Even the simplest piece of art benefits from a frame, but picture framers can charge a fortune. It is quite simple to take control of your own artwork and design your frames.

Use clip glass frames or cheap wooden frames as a starting point for your own design. You can use a glue gun to stick twigs, string, leaves, or other items to the glass or frame. Normal giftwrap can be used as a backing.

A fun postcard is framed with glued-on toy lizards.

You can use zippers, corrugated cardboard, suspenders, or anything you think would be fun.

Rope wound loosely and glued to the frame produces a suitably nautical feel.

Attach bay leaves with thumbtacks.

the art of
laminating

Hiding in the corner of most copy centers is the laminating machine. It can be put to better use than sealing conference badges and membership cards. Try this versatile technique for yourself.

A laminate is made of two sheets of clear plastic sealed together with heat. You can take a design made of any thin material like photocopies, ribbon, or tissue paper to a copy center and they will laminate it for you.

You can use laminates for placemats, coasters or backsplashes for bathrooms and kitchens. At about $1.50 for an 8½ x 11" sheet, laminate is one of the cheapest ways to create something new for your home.

Try using a series of laminates in front of a window. Punch holes, then insert key rings to hold together laminated sheets of tissue paper; hang the completed design from cup hooks.

Torn aluminum foil is laminated, wrapped around an old lampshade, and glued in place.

turning the
tables

A small table makes an appearance in nearly every home. Give yours a touch of style.

A circular piece of plastic-coated fabric, trimmed with pompons, can give your table a removable stain-proof surface.

Spray your table with metallic silver paint. Apply a coat of acrylic varnish and sprinkle on glitter and sequins. Allow to dry, then seal the design with two more coats of varnish. Place a sheet of glass on top for extra protection.

For this wrapped design you first need to cover your table with double-sided tape. Next wind ribbon around the table legs, center column, and top. Protect your table top edge with a circular piece of glass.

① Unfinished wood needs to be lightly sanded and given a coat of acrylic primer before painting.

② Use latex flat paint for a base color.

③ Cut out fun designs from giftwrap.

④ Stick your cutouts to the table with water-based white glue.

⑤ Satin-finish acrylic varnish will help the design survive more than occasional wear and tear.

TIP

● The more you use a table, the more coats of varnish you will need to protect the design.

dyeing for a change

A change of color can make an old piece of fabric look completely new. Dyeing sofa throws, pillow covers, bed linens, curtains, or any soft fabric is much cheaper than throwing out old and buying new. It is a solution to be considered when you feel the need for a change.

Fabric dyes come in an enormous range of colors, but bear in mind that, for example, a red dye will not turn a yellow or a green piece of cloth red. The color on the package will be absolutely true only for dyeing white fabric.

A tie-dyed throw gives an abstract effect.

Machine-wash dyes are very popular because they are easy to use.

You can also use dye to bring different colors to one piece of fabric. Tie rubber bands around a piece of cloth before dyeing, or tie the cloth itself into a knot. This will prevent dye from reaching all the material, giving you the chance to create more interesting tie-dye effects.

Expert help from dye manufacturers is available; a contact telephone number is listed at the back of the book.

Ottoman or sofa covers can be dyed.

trade s

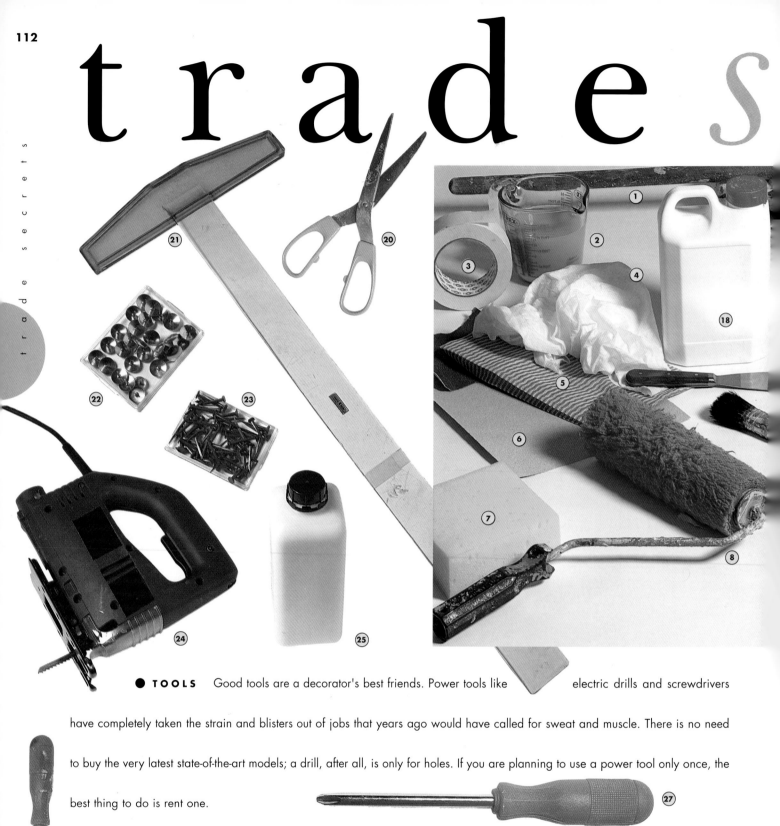

● **TOOLS** Good tools are a decorator's best friends. Power tools like electric drills and screwdrivers have completely taken the strain and blisters out of jobs that years ago would have called for sweat and muscle. There is no need to buy the very latest state-of-the-art models; a drill, after all, is only for holes. If you are planning to use a power tool only once, the best thing to do is rent one.

Be wary of so-called specialized decorating tools. If someone is trying to sell you a decorating sponge for $5 they are ripping you off. Use an inexpensve bath sponge. Top-of-the-line paintbrushes are not necessary. One roller, a large brush and a small one are all you usually need.

PAINT CHARTS

BASEBOARDS	▮ ✖ □
BATHROOM WALLS	★
BATHTUB (EXTERIOR)	✖ □ ■
CANE FURNITURE	● ■
CEILING	★
CHILDREN'S FURNITURE	● ▮
CHILDREN'S TOYS	○
COFFEE TABLE	● ▮ ■
CORRUGATED PLASTIC	▮ ✖ ■
CUPBOARD	● ▮ ✖
DINING TABLE	● ▮ ■
DOOR	▮ ✖ □
DOOR HANDLES	▮ ✖ □ ■ ●
FIREPLACE	● ▮ ✖ □
FLOOR - WOOD	● ◆
FLOOR - CONCRETE	◆
FLOOR - VINYL	● ◆
HEARTH	● ▮ ✖ □
KITCHEN WALLS	★ ●
KITCHEN CABINETS	▮ ✖ □
LAMP BASE - WOOD	● ▮ ■
LAMPSHADE	★ ● ■
PICTURE FRAME	★ ● ▮ ✖ □ ■
PAINTED RUG	●
REFRIGERATOR	▮ ✖ □ ■ ▲
STAIR HANDRAIL	▮ ✖ □ ■
STAIR TREADS	● ◆
SCREEN	●
SHELF	● ▮ ✖
STENCIL	● ■
TOILET SEAT	● ■
WARDROBE	● ▮ ✖ □ ■
WINDOW FRAMES	▮ ✖ □

Symbol	Type	PAINT FINISH	PAINT BASE	CLEAN EQUIPMENT WITH
★	LATEX FLAT PAINT	MATTE	WATER	WATER
●	LATEX FLAT PAINT SEALED WITH ACRYLIC VARNISH	*	WATER	WATER
▮	LATEX EGGSHELL	SLIGHT SHEEN	WATER	WATER
✖	OIL-BASED PAINT, EGGSHELL SATINWOOD	SLIGHT SHEEN	OIL	MINERAL SPIRITS
□	OIL-BASED PAINT, GLOSS	HIGH SHEEN	OIL	MINERAL SPIRITS
◆	FLOOR PAINT	HIGH SHEEN	OIL	MINERAL SPIRITS
■	SPRAY PAINT	HIGH SHEEN	OIL	MINERAL SPIRITS
○	NON-TOXIC	MATTE/SHEEN	WATER	WATER
▲	METAL PRIMER	MATTE/SHEEN	OIL	MINERAL SPIRITS

* see varnish chart on page 122

WHERE POSSIBLE, USE WATER-BASED PAINTS AND VARNISHES AS THESE ARE MORE ENVIRONMENTALLY FRIENDLY

ecrets

● **PREPARATION**   You've bought the paint and you can't wait to slosh it on your walls. Be warned, if you don't prepare properly you will never get a perfect finish and within a year whatever you do will start to look shoddy. You must sand down bumps and fill in cracks. If you are stripping wallpaper, make sure to get those nasty bits that just don't want to come off the wall. Preparation is a hugely important part of decorating, so don't believe the voice in your head telling you not to bother. Protect floors and furniture with drop cloths. A simple bed sheet will not protect your carpet from stray drops of paint because it will seep through, so use a special drop cloth or lay plastic sheeting under a bed sheet. Drop cloths and plastic sheeting are available from home-improvement stores, and it's easier to fold up a cloth than clean paint from your carpet.

● **GLOVES & CLOTHES**   Many paints are toxic, and scrubbing even a tiny bit of paint from your fingernails is a boring task, so always wear rubber gloves when painting. Choose a larger size of gloves than you think you need. If you are painting for any length of time your hands will need to breathe, and the larger paint-splattered gloves are easier to remove. No matter how hard you try or how small an amount of paint you are using, paint *will* get on your clothes. Paint can tell if you are in your finery and will choose this moment to drip, splatter, or smudge. Never paint in clothes you care about. Don't wear woolly socks or jumpers as fluff will stick to paint and varnish. Cotton is the best fabric for decorating in. If you have long hair, always tie it back before painting. Keep your hair out of the paint and the paint out of your hair.

● **FILLING A CRACK**   First gouge out the crack with a screwdriver. Making the crack larger might sound bizarre, but you will need to remove bits of plaster that may not look cracked, but are almost certainly damaged. Traditional powder filler, which you mix yourself with water, is far better than ready-mixed filler which is more difficult to sand. Mix the filler with water and then push it firmly into the crack with a spatula. Once the filler is completely dry, sand down the surface with sandpaper.

trade*s*

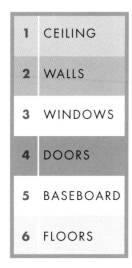

● **COVERING A WATERMARK**   Don't bother eliminating damp patches until you have found where the moisture has come from, and solve this problem before you do anything else. Allow the area to dry fully, which could take several days. Spray or brush on a stain blocker (available from paint stores). When the suface is dry, paint it back to its original color.

● **FIXING PEELING PAINT**   Peeling usually occurs when moisture has been trapped between the raw surface and the paint layer. Scrape off any loose flakes, sand down to the raw surface, prime, and paint.

● **WHERE TO START PAINTING IN A ROOM**   Follow the numbers on the sketch when you are painting a room.

1	CEILING
2	WALLS
3	WINDOWS
4	DOORS
5	BASEBOARD
6	FLOORS

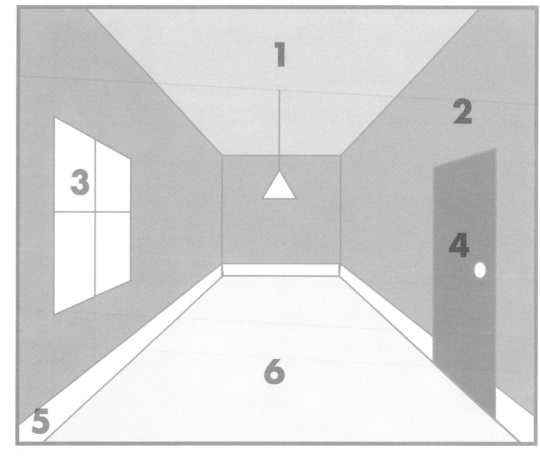

● **SANDPAPER AND PREPARING A SURFACE** The most common uses of sandpaper are to eliminate lumps and to prepare certain surfaces for painting. The type or grade of paper used depends on how much material you need to remove. Rougher paper, graded 40 or 60, is the heavy-duty stuff for big lumps, while the high-grade paper, 100 to 200, is for finer work. You will often need two grades, starting with a low-grade and finishing off with a high-grade paper. Take special care to brush or vacuum up dust after sanding; otherwise it will get in your paint and spoil the finish.

● **PRIMER** Primer is magic stuff, vital if you are planning on painting over unfinished wood, new plaster, or synthetic surfaces like kitchen cabinets. It absorbs resin and helps bond paint to the surface, which stops the top coat from flaking. If you omit a primer coat you are making a serious mistake. You can use acrylic primer underneath either oil-based or water-based paint.

● **PAINT** Most cans of paint resist attempts at invasion, but don't resort to gouging at the lid in desperation. Even if you do eventually force a lid open, you will never persuade a gouged-out lid to fit properly again. Paint can lids must be gently levered out with something like a flathead screwdriver; keep moving around the rim of the can, levering as you go. Always stir paint thoroughly each time you open a can. This ensures an even blend of color. When pouring paint into another container, be careful not to cover the name of the paint with drips. It's an annoying mistake no one ever makes more than once: some day you'll need another can of that exact shade of green — if only you could remember what it was called. Alternatively, write the name of the paint on the lid of the can.

● **MASKING TAPE** You can use masking tape to separate paint colors with a straight edge or to paint stripes on surfaces. As you stick it on, run your finger hard along the side of the tape that will come up against wet paint. This prevents paint from bleeding under the tape and ruining your design. Paint *away* from masking tape, making sure that bristles don't go under the tape. The best time to remove

trades

masking tape is when the paint is half dry. If the paint is completely dry, the tape will tear; if too wet, paint will run. Peel off the masking tape gently, at an angle away from the wet paint. (If you are worried about masking tape lifting the paint finish when you remove it, first rub the strips of masking tape against cotton clothing, sticky side down, to get rid of some of the stickiness before using it. This will prevent spoiling the paint.)

● **PAINTING WITH A BRUSH**   Brushes are ideal for small areas and for getting into corners where a roller cannot reach. Avoid the cheapest brushes, which can shed, and choose a medium-priced one with tightly packed bristles. Buy top-of-the-line only if you are going to be decorating on a daily basis. Paint needs to be worked onto a surface, so don't always brush in one direction. For large, flat surfaces use a roller where possible.

● **DEBUGGING PAINT**   Bugs, hair, and dust can ruin the most carefully painted piece of work, so be careful. If you notice something swimming in the paint pot, dip in a brush near the poor little bug, and as you remove the brush the insect should come with it. If you notice a only bug once you have applied your paint, use a damp cloth to wipe the area down and start painting all over again. To remove grit from a can of paint, filter it into a new container using a sieve or an old pair of stockings.

● **CLEANING A BRUSH**   Like shoes, brushes will get worn in, so once you find a brush you love, treat it well. Clean it properly and hang it upside down to dry and store, and it will serve you well for many years. Cleaning up is the worst part of any job, and it is tempting to leave dirty paintbrushes until the next day. Resist. The longer you leave paint to dry into bristles, the harder it is to clean. If you don't clean your brushes properly, old paint will come back to haunt you as you begin your next project. You can make the job as easy as 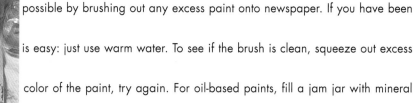 possible by brushing out any excess paint onto newspaper. If you have been using water-based paint, cleaning is easy: just use warm water. To see if the brush is clean, squeeze out excess water, and if it still shows the color of the paint, try again. For oil-based paints, fill a jam jar with mineral

ecrets

spirits to above the level of the bristles, dunk the brush in, use the inside lip of the jar to wipe the excess off the brush, then wipe on newspaper. Once you have done this a number of times, pour dishwashing liquid right inside the brush and rinse clean with water. If you are going to use 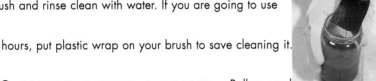 the same oil-based paint within 24 hours, put plastic wrap on your brush to save cleaning it.

● **PAINTING WITH A ROLLER** Rollers need to be soaked in  paint. Try to get as much paint onto the roller as possible, without having it drip. Don't try to cover too large an area with one application of paint as the roller dries out and the paint will look streaky. Make sure you roll in various directions, not just back and forth. Don't re-roll a wet paint surface, as this will lift the paint. If you are painting too quickly and don't come to a complete halt before you lift the roller from the wall, you will spin the roller, sending tiny specks of paint everywhere. Small rollers are ideal for the doors of kitchen cabinets.

TIP   When painting high ceilings, or floors, try using an old broomstick as an extension for your roller handle.

● **CLEANING A ROLLER** You can use a stick to get rid of excess paint in a roller. Slide the stick down the length of the roller as tightly as you can, and force it down the length to squeeze out the paint, preferably over a paint tray. Hold the roller close against a bathtub faucet to keep splashing to a minimum. Run your fingers through the roller to disperse the paint, and spin the roller around under the water. Remove the roller cover from the handle and wash away all the remaining paint. Rinse thoroughly, place the roller sleeve back on the handle and spin to remove the last traces of water. Remove the roller cover again and leave it upright to dry. Incidentally, never buy a roller with a non-detachable cover, for you will never get it truly clean.

trades

● **HOW TO MIX COLORWASH** Colorwashes are thinned paints and can be used to break up flat color. If you want to see a second shade behind a top color, or want to create a dreamy effect on a wall, you need a colorwash. There's no need to buy an expensive one from a store—make your own. Use a plastic pitcher or any clear transparent container to mix your wash in. Dilute one part latex flat paint to four parts of water. Diluting a paint doesn't affect its color; it just makes it more transparent, so don't choose a darker or lighter shade than you want, because water doesn't affect the hue.

● **HOW TO APPLY COLORWASH**  Once you have a dry coat of latex flat, either an old coat or one you've freshly painted, you can slosh on the wash with a brush or rag. For washes it is especially important to keep your brush or rag strokes irregular and heading in all directions. Colorwash dries quickly, so speed is of the essence.

● **PAINTING WITH A BAG** You don't need to limit your painting to rollers and brushes. Try plastic bags, paper towels, plastic wrap, waxed paper, anything. Different brush substitutes will give you different paint finishes.

 ● **PAINTING OVER WALLPAPER** If you can't face stripping off old wallpaper, then you can paint straight over it with latex flat paint. This is suitable for both smooth and embossed papers.

● **BLOW-DRYER** A blow-dryer will speed up the drying time 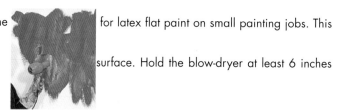 for latex flat paint on small painting jobs. This is ideal when stenciling or applying more than one color to a surface. Hold the blow-dryer at least 6 inches away from the painted surface, or the paint will begin to crack.

● **STORING PAINT** Paint forms a skin when left for more than a month and becomes more difficult to use. The best way to stop this is to store (well-sealed) cans upside down. This way the skin forms on the bottom of the can, out of harm's way.

● **WOODSTAINS** Most inexpensive wood furniture is made from pine, which has a fresh, pale color. However, if you long for the deep rich color of a wood like mahogany, you don't need to spend a fortune or worry about rainforest conservation; simply treat with a woodstain. You can match the color of any wood you desire with commercially available woodstains. Stir carefully and brush on the stain like a varnish. For colors like this eyecatching blue, you will need to mix your own stain. Mix together one part latex flat paint to two parts water and stir thoroughly. Apply with a damp rag or brush and after 20–30 seconds use a damp, pure cotton cloth or old cotton T-shirt to wipe off any excess stain. This allows the grain of the wood to show through the color. Once the stain is completely dry, seal with acrylic varnish. If you are not sure how deep a stain you want, wipe off any excess even more quickly than you would do normally. You can apply many more coats if you want to build up the color, but you can't undo mistakes without sanding back to bare wood.

● **GLUE** Decorators need white glue for glueing cutout designs, spray glue for holding stencils in place, and a glue gun for heavier objects. If you use a spray glue, wear a face mask and always keep windows and doors open.

● **HOW TO VARNISH** The first few strokes of paint color on a blank expanse of wall are always fun. Unfortunately varnish has none of this excitement. It's a dull job, but without it your carefully completed work will chip, fray, and wear. Varnishing is always time well spent. Acrylic varnish is much better than other varieties; it is water-based, easy to clean, and dries far faster than polyurethane varnish, so you can apply many more coats in a day. Varnish doesn't necessarily mean shiny. Matte, satin, and gloss finishes are available, and you should choose the varnish according to the design you want to protect. Never shake a can of varnish. If you do, air bubbles will form, and once there, they will transfer to your surface. Just stir gently. When you first apply the surface

trades

varnish use crisscross strokes to work the varnish onto the surface, then 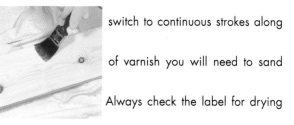 switch to continuous strokes along the line of any grain; let each coat dry thoroughly. In between each coat of varnish you will need to sand lightly with a very fine sandpaper, making sure to remove all dust. Always check the label for drying times, and be careful of using central heating to speed up the process. A radiator can dry the surface of a wet coat of varnish, but underneath the varnish may still be wet, and like half-dry nail polish, it will ripple up.

● **THE VARNISH CHART**

The number of coats needed depends on the amount of wear and tear the object will get. Use this table as a guide.

TO PROTECT	COATS	TO PROTECT	COATS
WALL DESIGN	1	COFFEE TABLE	4
LAMPSHADE	1	HEARTH	4
FIREPLACE	1	CHILDREN'S FURNITURE	4
SCREEN	1	BOOKCASE	4
EXTERIOR OF BATHTUB	2	BATHROOM CABINETS	5
HOPE CHEST	2	KITCHEN CABINETS	5
CHEST OF DRAWERS	2	KITCHEN BACKSPLASH	5 – 8
HANDRAIL	3	WOOD FLOOR	5 – 10
CHAIRS	3	STAIRS	5 – 10
DINING TABLE	4	PAINTED RUGS OR DESIGNS ON FLOORS	10

The finish you get depends on the type of acrylic varnish that is used.

FLAT ACRYLIC VARNISH *GIVES A MATTE FINISH.*

EGGSHELL ACRYLIC VARNISH *GIVES A SLIGHT SHEEN FINISH.*

GLOSS ACRYLIC VARNISH *GIVES A HIGH SHEEN FINISH.*

ecrets

● **STENCILING** Remountable spray adhesive should be used to keep the stencil in place. Masking tape may be used, but it's not as effective as remountable spray. The spray holds the stencil firmly in place, and you can peel the stencil off and smooth it down again without needing to reach continually for the spray can. Using spray glue stops paint from leaking under stencils far better than tape. The best way to stencil is with a synthetic sponge. Use large pieces for big stencils and smaller bits for more delicate work. The secret to successful stenciling is to use as little paint as possible. Work out excess paint onto a piece of cardboard until there is virtually no paint left on the sponge, then dab gently over the stencil.

● **FABRIC** There's no need to spend lots of money on expensive fabrics for soft furnishings like curtains, cushion covers, and throws when felt, muslin, dress and lining fabrics are readily available and inexpensive.

● **THE ENVIRONMENT—BE AWARE!** Whenever possible use materials that cause the least amount of damage to the environment. Forget about mahogany, ebony, teak, and African walnut; using these in your home is irresponsible. Where possible use lumber carrying the FSC Trademark—an international symbol that indicates lumber and lumber products from a well-managed source. Water-based and acrylic paints and varnishes are preferable to oil-based ones. Oil-based paints contain solvents, as does mineral spirits, and both are environmentally damaging. Never dispose of solvents down the drain and into the water system. Put them in clearly labeled, old paint cans and contact your local government regarding their disposal. Don't throw away your old bath and kitchen fixtures because somebody somewhere can use them. Charities and associations for the homeless are always looking for old kitchen cabinets, bathroom fixtures, light fixtures, etc. When you're painting, re-use materials as much as possible: buy one pair of tough rubber gloves rather than a pack of lightweight disposable ones; use rags rather than paper towels; buy re-useable rather than disposable items. For more information contact Greenpeace at (202) 462-1177.

where to *shop*

Paint and Art Supplies

FLAX ART & DESIGN
1699 Market Street
San Francisco
CA 94103
t: **415-552-2355**

HOBBIES CO OF SAN FRANCISCO
5150 Geary Boulevard
San Francisco
CA 94122
t: **415-386-2802**

PAINT EFFECTS
materials and instruction
2426 Fillmore Street
San Francisco
CA 94115
t: **415-292-7780**
www.painteffects.com

TEXAS ART SUPPLY
2001 Montrose
Houston
TX 77006
t: **713-526-5221**

PEARL PAINT CO., INC.
308 Canal Street
New York
NY 10013
t: **212-431-7932**

CHARETTE FAVOR RUHL
31 Olympia Ave.
Woburn
MA 01888
t: **800-367-3729**
Call for other Northeast locations

SAM FLAX ART SUPPLIES
Atlanta, GA: *t:* **404-3527200**
Orlando, FL: *t:* **407-898-9785**

GUIRY'S, INC.
2468 South Colorado Boulevard
Denver
CO 80222
t: **303-758-8244**

Architectural Salvage

*These stores tend to have
wide price ranges—don't be
put off by the $500.00 door;
you can find good buys.*

URBAN ORE
1333 Sixth Street
Berkeley
CA 94710
t: **510-559-4454**

OHMEGA SALVAGE
2407 San Pablo Ave.
Berkeley
CA 94702
t: **510-843-7368**

UNITED HOUSE WRECKING
535 Hope Street
Stamford
CT 06906
t: **203-548-5371**

GREAT GATSBY'S
5070 Peachtree Industrial Boulevard
Atlanta
GA 30341
t: **770-457-1903**

MATERIALS UNLIMITED
2 W. Michigan Ave.
Ypsilanti
MI 48197
t: **313-483-6980**

RENOVATION SOURCE
3512 N. Southport
Chicago
IL 60657
t: **773-327-1250**

ZIGGURAT'S
1702 N. Milwaukee Ave.
Chicago
IL 60647
t: **773-227-6290**

THE EMPORIUM
2515 Morse Street
Houston
TX 77019
t: **713-528-3808**

CORONADO SALVAGE
4200 Broadway, SE
Albuquerque
NM 87105
t: **505-877-2821**

**QUEEN CITY ARCHITECTURAL
SALVAGE**
4750 Brighton Boulevard
Denver
CO 80216
t: **303-296-0925**

THE ARCHITECTURAL BANK
1824 Felicity Street
New Orleans
LA 70113
t: **504-523-2702**

where to *shop*

**OLD THEATER
ARCHITECTURAL SALVAGE**
2045 Broadway
Kansas City
MO 64108
t: **816-283-3740**

**ARCHITECTURAL ANTIQUES
EXCHANGE**
715 N. Second Street
Philadelphia
PA 19123
t: **215-922-3669**

Stencils

THE ITINERANT STENCILER
11030 173rd Street, S.E.
Renton
WA 98059
t: **206-226-0306**

AMERICAN HOME STENCILS
10007 South 76th Street
Franklin
WI 53132
t: **414-425-5381**

AMERICAN TRADITIONAL STENCILS
Bow Street
RD 281
Northwood
NH 03261
t: **603-942-8100**

STENCILERS EMPORIUM
P.O. Box 536
Twinsburg
OH 44087
t: **216-425-1766**

STENCIL EASE
P.O. Box 1127
Old Saybrook
CT 06475
t: **203-395-0150**

Moldings and Millwork

**ARMSTRONG WORLD
INDUSTRIES DESIGN**
Resource Center
Box 8022
Plymouth
MI 48170-9948
t: **800-704-8000**

GEORGIA-PACIFIC
t: **800-284-5347**

RAYMOND ENKEBOLL DESIGNS
16506 Avalon Boulevard
Carson
CA 90746
t: **310-532-1400**

*For a zinc backsplash: Once you know how
much metal you need, look under "zinc" in
the yellow pages for a wholesale distributor.
After buying the raw sheets, find a "metal
fabricator" (also in your local yellow pages)
who will cut them to size.*

Miscellaneous

SUNSET CARPETS
carpet workroom
2411 Harrison Street
San Francisco
CA 94110
t: **415-643-1900**

CLIFF'S VARIETY
hardware, fabrics, crafts, variety
479 Castro
San Francisco
CA 94114
t: **415-431-5365**

BARCLAY'S LEAF IMPORTS, INC.
gold leaf and gilding supplies
21 Wilson Terrace
Elizabeth
NJ 07208
t: **908-353-5522**

ELAINE'S RAGS
chenille bedlinens
1010 36th Street
Des Moines
IA 50311
t: **515-255-8714**

OLE CHARLESTON FORGE
custom iron work
970 Morrison Drive
Charleston
SC 29403
t: **803-723-3816**

TAP PLASTICS
plastic cut to size
154 South Van Ness Ave.
San Francisco
CA 94110
t: **415-864-7360**

BELL'OCCHIO
antique and unusual ribbons
8 Brady Street
San Francisco
CA 94103
t: **415-864-4048**

index

index

acknowledgments

Authors' *Acknowledgments*

Extra special thanks to...

Colin Poole for his patience, wit, and Lassie Come Home impressions; Annabelle Poole for keeping Colin in line; Kes James for the use of the expression "nightmare"; Jeremy Gordon for the introduction to the BBC and everything else; Anthea Morton-Saner for believing in the book; Daisy Goodwin for giving me new horizons; Wesley Bolton for turning my drawings into wonderful realities; Judith Burton for being the best there is; Kathleen Duffy for the encouragement; Debbie Semon for lending an ear; Katrina Sandlin for being as big as they come.

Without whom...

Andy Batt & Martin, Todd Bolton, Martin Butler, Audrey Carden, John Duckworth, Greg Demosthenous, Keith Fuller, Frank Farci, Alan Firman, Louise Holgate, Molly Johnson, Dominic Luscombe, Gail MacGregor, Michael Penford, Scott Phillips, Alison Pearce, Tony Randel, Seiriol Tomos, Rikki Tamrat, Caroline Tyler, Barbara Vidal-Hall.

Into their homes...

Diane & Andrew Holmes, Patsy Youngstein, Sascha O'Hagan, Sam Morse, Kate & Kristan Stone, Rachel & Izzy Selly, Karen McGill, Fiona Cole, Tonia Nagel, Russel Denton, Louise & Tom Walsh, Jaimie & Louise, Claire Mulley, Susan Campbell, Brian & Emma Wares.

Thanks to...

Pamela Anderson, Paula Bridges, Katy Eachus, Lorna Frame, Kaye Godleman, Asif Hasan, Elaine Hill, Diana Henry, Tommy & Jaqui Hopkins, Sascha Jeffrey, Janine Josman, Anvar Khan, Ariane Koek, Geraldine McClelland, Trisha O'Leary, B. Orlando; Pat, John, Pauline and everyone at Crispins; Richard Peskin, Patricia Rutherford, Joey Searle, Marguerite Smith, S. Tripoda, Helen Williams of Stencil Library, Simon Morris at Texas/Homebase; Colin Mitchell Rose at Craig & Rose; Leyland Paints - Edgware Road; Evelyn Strout at John Lewis; William at Ikea; Purves & Purves, Samantha at the Water Monopoly; David Mackay of Signs & Designs; Dylon; Plasterworks; Lakeland Plastics; Jonathon Pellegrini.

Goods supplied by...

African Escape: page 57 (tribal art); Stencil Library: pages 19 (zebra), 22 (rug border), 28 (tiles), 39 (mosaic), 48 (leaf), 55 (tiles), 64 (floor tile), 79 (hearth & column), 80 (fleur-de-lys), 92 (laurel wreath), 96 (flying pigs), 102 (bees), 123 (train); Lynne Robinson & Richard Lowther: page 23 from Stencilling Book; Texas/Homebase Kitchens: pages 38 & 48; Water Monopoly: inspiration for pages 60 & 61; Sophie Chandler: page 19 (bottle light); Helen Allen: page 24 (pouffe); Robert Wyatt: page 13 (lamp); Purves & Purves: page 13 (sofas); Elephant: page 13 (cushions, coffee table, and accessories); Linzi Hodges: page 13 (glass bottles); Sue Magee: page 13 (glass dish); Ikea: page 13 (rug); Plasterworks: page 18 (head); Santoro Design: pages 43, 87, 106, 107, 109 (giftwrap); Penny Kennedy Design: pages 30,31 (giftwrap); Trumpet Design: page 57 (card); Paperchase: pages 87, 106, 107 (giftwraps); John Lewis: page 84 (glass); David Mackay: page 105 (sailor giftwrap); Dylon dyes were used throughout the book. The varnishes and floor paints used throughout this book were supplied by Craig & Rose.

Photographs

All the following photographs by Colin Poole:

Pages 13, 14, 15, 16, 17, 18, 19, 20, 21, 22, 23, 24, 25, 28, 34, 35, 36, 38, 39, 40, 41, 42, 43, 44, 45, 46, 47, 48, 49, 50, 51, 52, 53, 55, 59, 64, 65, 66, 68, 69, 70, 71, 72, 73, 74, 75, 78, 80, 81, 82, 83, 84, 85, 86, 87, 88, 89, 90, 91, 92, 93, 97, 103, 105, 107, 110. © 1996 Anne McKevitt.

Pages 2, 3, 4, 5, 6, 7, 10, 11, 12, 29, 30, 31, 56, 57, 62, 63, 67, 76, 77, 94, 95, 98, 99, 100, 101, 102, 106, 107, 108, 109, 114, 115, 116, 117, 118, 119, 120, 121. © 1996 Anne McKevitt & Shelley Warrington.

Pages 32, 33, 79, 96, 104, 111, 112, 113. © 1996 Shelley Warrington.

Additional photography of Anne McKevitt's designs:

Capitol Photographs: pages; 36, 44 (after), 55, 69, 85.
Chris Wood: pages 20, 21 (before), 66 (before), 68, 88 (before & after), 89 (before).
Kitchens, Bedrooms & Bathrooms/Steve Hawkins: page 85 (main shot).

The publishers wish to thank the photographers and organizations for their kind permission to reproduce the following photographs in this book:

Belle Magazine/Sharrin Rees: pages 8-9; Vogue Living/Simon Kenny: page 13 above; Antoine Bootz (designer Dana Nicholson) pages 26-27; Lavinia Press: page 27 above and below; World of Interiors/Jonathan Lovekin: page 27 center; Jerome Darblay (Jean-Jacques Ory): page 37; La Casa de Marie Claire/Edouardo Munoz: page 54; Elizabeth Whiting & Associates/Mark Luscombe-Whyte: page 58; Robert Harding Picture Library/Country Homes & Interiors IPC MAgazines/Polly Wreford: pages 60-61.